The Two of Us

Intimate Conversations in My Quiet Time with God

by
Shelly Pettibone

*Martha,
Be comforted and inspired!
Peace and Joy,
Shelly Pettibone*

Copyright © 2018
By Shelly Pettibone
All rights reserved.

ISBN-13: 978-1985347267
ISBN-10: 1985347261

Dedications

My prayer for myself as I write this book ~

> *"Free your paper with the breathing of your heart."*
>
> *~ William Wordsworth ~*

My prayer for those who read this book ~

> *Your relationship with God, Jesus, and the Holy Spirit will be touched and changed by the conversations and writings in this book.*

Special Thanks to

Susan List for the Illustrations

Sara Otto for the Cover Design

Natalie Sum, Maureen Lilleeng, and Sean Pettibone for the Editing

Richard Trigilio for Publishing Project Management

Gratitudes

Writing this book has been a 17 year journey. It began with God and me and has, over the years, been accompanied by beautiful and gifted people who have been instrumental in making this book a reality.

I would first like to thank my wonderful husband, Sean. He has been a great support to me emotionally and technologically. In 2000, when I originally started to write my book, he helped me with all the computer and technical issues that came with it. From 2002 on, the book writing process was dormant. Then in 2017, I sensed God asking me to start writing again. Through those 15 years came two house moves and three new computer purchases. I didn't even know if we would be able to find my manuscript on our current computer. I was feeling that if God wanted me to write again, He would help me find my manuscript. Sean spent several days looking for it with no success. Then, on one last night, he gave it another try. I was starting to get nervous about the possibility of not finding my manuscript. Then God's presence gently filled me as He spoke to my heart, "Be at peace." Literally, not more than five minutes passed and Sean said, "Shelly, come here. Is this what you are looking for?" And there was my manuscript on our computer screen just as I had left it in 2002!

Thank you also to my two beautiful daughters, Ashley Humphrey and Shannon Olandese, for always being my cheerleaders. To my wonderful sons-in-law, Elliot and Tom, thank you for your kind words of support.

Because I've never written a book before, I had no idea whether to self-publish or have a publishing company do it. I thought about both options, talked to a lot of people and read a lot of information about it. I decided to let God open a door for me either way.

My Aunt Barbara Willis, who is a self-published author of several books, inspired me to think about writing and having a story to tell. Her beautiful style of writing helped me think of what kind of style I might have. I talked with her at our 2017 family reunion about her writing journey and how to self-publish a book. It was fun to hear her story. She said to me, "I am so happy you are writing a book. But the person you really need to talk to about self-publishing is your Uncle Dick because he also has self-published books and helped me every step of the way with mine."

When I talked to my Uncle Dick Trigilio (Aunt Barbara's brother-in-law) he too was excited for me. He explained to me a bit about how the process would work. Then came his words I'll always remember, "If you want, I would be happy to help you with your self-publishing from A-Z." I think my jaw dropped open. I truly felt like this was the door God wanted me to walk through. I instantaneously said, "Yes! I can't tell you what an answer to prayer this is." From that point on, he has been with me every step of the way. I could not have done this without him.

My friend, Natalie Sum, helped me tremendously with the editing of this book. She has also been a true cheerleader every step of the way by helping me keep my timeline.

One day before I was to meet Natalie for lunch, I received an email that the person I had talked to about doing the illustrations for my book was unable to do them. I was a bit disappointed but trusted that God would bring someone else into my journey. As Natalie and I began to discuss my book writing progress, I told her about my email and said, "I really don't have any other illustrator leads." Then she said, "I have a friend who does watercolor pictures, and if you want, I can see if she is interested in your project." Enter Susan List.

Susan is an amazing artist and the illustrator of the beautiful artwork you see in this book. I wanted my illustrations to be soft watercolors and that is exactly what she loves to do. I so enjoyed working with her and am blessed by her artistic gifts.

Jessica Ptaszek has been my good friend for many years. Her part in this journey was helping me with the photo shoot for the picture on the cover of this book. We went to the Bellermine Jesuit Retreat Center in Barrington, Illinois to take pictures on their beautiful grounds. This retreat center is where I spend many of my quiet times with God. She helped me carry the bench that you see on the cover to a forested area. We had a lot of laughs because neither one of us had ever done this before. We hoped that after all the pictures we took, at least one would be usable. The picture you see on the cover is what was chosen.

I also would like to thank my three dear friends, Sue Clinger, Melodee Cook, and Susie Allison, for their continued support and encouragement throughout my writing process. They have encouraged me to think outside the box in living out my dream of what God has called me to do in writing this book.

Thank you all!

Shelly Pettibone

Journal Entries

Introduction xiii

How to Read This Book xvi

Lord, Prepare My Heart
    for Beginnings xviii

Journal Entries for Beginnings

    You Are a Somebody to Me 3
    Shine Your Light 5
    Pondering My Light 6
    The Journey Begins 9
    My First Encounter with Jesus 11
    A Seed of Compassion 12
    The Embrace 15
    My Desire 18
    Growing Older 21
    My First Love 22
    The Gift 23
    In the Beginning 24
    Behold Me Beholding You 28
    Lord, Prepare My Heart
        to Praise You 30

Journal Entries for Praise

    I Love Your Praises 35
    Praise You from Your Word 36
    Beautiful Creation 38
    Melody of Delight 39
    Room for Praise 40
    Praise You for Your Character 41
    Praise You from My Heart 45
    Praise You for This Day 46
    Lord, Prepare My Heart for Prayer 48

Journal Entries for Prayer

Secret Place of Prayer 54
The Stillness 55
It's Enough 56
Prayer Steps 58
Where You Lead Me 59
Safety in Prayer 62
Acceptance 63
One in Prayer 65
The Lake 66
Joy 67
My Ears, My Eyes 68
Unbelief Turns to Faith 69
Rescuing 70
In Need of a Savior 72
Lord, Prepare My Heart
    for Confession 74

Journal Entries for Confession

As I Acknowledge My Sins, Oh,
    How You Love Me, God 80
The Wound of Sin 82
Better Than Thanks Sometimes 84
Heart of Forgiveness 85
God's Gaze 87
Sin Is Not My Friend 89
The Cross 90
New Mercies 93
Lord, Prepare My Heart for Struggles 94

Journal Entries for Struggles

The Vessel 98
Dark Night of My Soul 101
My Shell 109
The Ocean 111
The Bud 113
Lord, Prepare My Heart to Listen 115

Journal Entries for Listening
    My Request 121
    Being Open 122
    Your Beautiful Voice, Lord, I Do Hear ...124
    Another Way to Hear Your Voice 126
    In My Favorite Chair 129
    Acknowledge Me 131
    The Silence of Listening 132
    The Pond 135
    The Statues 137
    Trust 139
    Lord, Prepare My Heart to Give
                You Thanks 140

Journal Entries for Thanksgiving
    Thanking God Through Scripture 145
    Thanking God from My Heart 147
    Lord, Prepare My Heart for Endings 152

Journal Entries for Endings
    My Tapestry 157
    Meadow on the Ledge 161
    Beyond the Trees 165
    Lord, Prepare My Heart
           for New Beginnings 166

Offerings to Ponder 169

Scripture References 171

Poems, Songs, and
        Quote References 173

Illustrations

Shine Your Light 4
Path of Beginnings 8
Wonder 10
The Embrace 14
Growing Older 20
Heart Praises 34
One in Prayer 64
My Offering 78
Dark Night 100
Growth Emerges 106
My Shell 108
Listening 120
Dance of Thanksgiving 144
Meadow on the Ledge 160
Beyond the Trees 164

Introduction

I am so excited that you are reading this book. It has always been my inmost desire for others to have a deeper relationship with God. Sharing about my relationship with Jesus is a part of that. God is showing me that the truest form of myself, the person God created me to be, is in sharing my relationship with Him to others.

The writings in this book are about my nearness with my first love, Jesus. It is not a documentary but a love story between God and me, to be read as a devotional of love letters expressed on paper—tender, vulnerable, intimate expressions. I hope this book inspires an abiding thirst between you and your Beloved.

This book has been 17 years in the making. Yes, that not only sounds like a long time, it is! I felt led to create a book that would contain the writings of my personal prayer journal. These journal entries were conversations between God and me. I would spend hours in quiet time with God during my formative years, learning how to pray and listen for His voice. I would write down my thoughts and when I felt God respond, either through Scripture or a revelation in my heart, I would write it down in words to describe it the best I could.

My early years of journaling consisted of experiences in my daily life, like a diary. As I got older, I journaled about God—who He was and where He was in my life. In my adulthood, journaling became more about my continued faith journey and growth in my awareness of my closeness with God.

I felt God leading me to make these original journal entries the basis for my book. Included with these journal entries are poems, song lyrics, quotes, Scripture, and beautiful artwork, adding color and life to my story. It's a devotional to be pondered in your heart as an offering of celebration and contemplation.

Not all 17 years were spent writing. It took me two years just to organize all my journal entries and put them in some sort of composition. Then, there was no activity at all. I felt absolutely no movement from God to work on my book. I wondered many times if this was a futile mission and if I originally heard God accurately about writing a book. Yet, during those years, I kept the book idea in my heart and did not let it go. Somehow, I felt this was real and that it was from God. Then, 15 years later, the book idea reemerged. I started getting renewed ideas and unique impressions for artwork to depict my years of journaling.

The concepts for the artwork evolved from me journaling as a young girl to me journaling as a mature woman. When you follow the artwork throughout the book you will notice that no matter what my age, my journal is near at hand. You will see a young woman finding her way into the heart of God through the intimacy of prayer, God's presence and contemplation. She starts as a girl, not knowing what prayer is, yet finding her way there through her strong desire to just be with God and experience Him deeply. This book is a compilation of precious moments made up of both joyful and difficult experiences I have had with Jesus in my beginning years of faith.

It is designed as a devotional for you to either read in chapter order or skip around as your heart leads. In this manner, it's a compilation of varied art forms for you to feel, hear, see, and sense God in the midst of the words and pictures.

My heart believes that God has plans for you as you read this book. I pray it deepens your relationship with Him and expands your heart and mind to prayer and the many ways you can hear His voice and experience Him deeply. My hope is that this devotional will move you deeper into what you already have with Jesus or create a stirring in you to start your journey into His nearness.

This is a love story. A great love story between my Jesus and me. *The Two of Us.*

I pray you find joy, intimacy, and depth in your relationship with Jesus as you read these conversations.

May God's gentle *kindness* and deep, unfailing *love,* fill your heart perfectly for you. He is, in this moment with you, smiling with delight and beholding you. Behold Him.

How to Read This Book

In order to get the most from this book, it is important to understand how it is organized.

There are eight chapters, each with its own color that helps to identify and set them apart.

Before each chapter starts, there is a section where I ask God to prepare my heart for the next step in my own heart journey.

Within each chapter are journal entries relating to the subject of the chapter.

The journal entries are conversations from my many years of journaling with God. These entries consist of quotes from my journaling, how I interpret God speaking to me in that moment and occasional comments from present day.

Within each journal entry, my voice is represented by regular text. God's responses are represented by italics. When I occasionally speak in the present moment, in explanation of an entry, it is represented in brackets.

Within each chapter are quotes from other people, song lyrics, and Scripture. These are all in black text.

There are several important themes running through the book.

1. God's promises to me, from the beginning, and consistently throughout my life, were to always be with me and always protect me.

2. God placed a love for others in need within my heart from an early age.

3. In my childhood, God pursued me and in turn I pursued Him.

4. God instilled in me early on, a love for journaling.

5. I find God in nature while journaling, especially in quiet places.

6. Peace and joy are deeply rooted in me.

7. I lacked a voice for the better part of my life and Jesus gave me a special voice to help others have a deeper relationship with Him. Writing is one of these voices.

At the end of this book are "Offerings," or questions, for you to ponder about what you have read in each chapter. They may be helpful to you in your own conversations with God. Journaling your thoughts may also be a way to deepen your awareness of God's presence as you contemplate the questions.

Feel free to read this book as a story, from beginning to end, or as individual devotionals, skipping around each journal entry.

If you read it as a story, you will find that each chapter is designed to take your soul on a journey through years of heartfelt conversations between Jesus and me.

Begin your heart journey now!

Lord, Prepare My Heart for Beginnings

Father, as I begin to write about my relationship with You from the first time I can remember You in my life, it all starts to come back to me in words and feelings. Take me back to the beginning, Lord, with You.

> "For I know the plans and thoughts that I have for you, says the Lord, plans for peace and well-being and not for disaster, to give you a future and a hope."
>
> Jeremiah 29:11
> Amplified Bible

Beginnings

†

When I think of my beginnings with You, God, I think of our love for each other. Lord, You have always been my first love. And always will be.

†

"With man this is impossible, but with God all things are possible."

Matthew 19:26
New International Version

You Are a Somebody to Me

Lord, as I think more and more about writing this book, I have even more questions. In the world of writing books, I am a nobody. I've never written a book before. No one knows me in the writing and publishing worlds. Nor do I know them. Technically, for me to write a book, expect someone to publish it and hope that someone will read it, feels impossible.

Lord, how will this be possible?

Then I hear You whisper to me gently,

You may be a nobody to them, but you are a somebody to Me.

Then something strangely seems possible about this whole idea.

Lord, when I think about who will read this book, I wonder if it will be few or many. I wonder if my book will change people's lives. The profitability I seek is in how many people are touched by the writings in this book.

With any amount, I can make it greater. Much greater. So do not worry about who or how many will read this book. I will take care of that. Pray that your hand, which writes, finds the words from your heart to speak in ways that reach others.

Shine Your Light

Shine Your Light

I love being in the forest with You on this bench, Lord. The quiet of nature fills my soul. I feel Your presence here and it brings me joy. I have so much to journal about. It's always been just You and me and my journal. The two of us. To tell my story of us feels a bit scary.

My dear one, it's okay to be scared. I am with you in your anxiousness. But know this, you were made to shine your light. The light in you is Me. The way I created you is how you express your light.

I want to be a light, Lord. I want to shine the light You have given me. I will be a light for You, Lord. It's time for me to share the two of us. I want You to know I feel peaceful and confident in You and what You are leading me to do, because I am confident it is You who is leading me.

You will shine a beautiful light, dear one. It's always been beautiful.

[I always felt, from a young age, that I had greater purpose in life than what I was living. What that was, I did not know. Now, in my 50's, I am living out the places in my heart in which I have always felt awareness of God. He has brought these heart places all together to form a specific calling—helping others experience a deeper relationship with God. Writing this book is how I can share my relationship with God to others. This is my voice. This is my light.]

Pondering My Light

Lord, this is what I am learning from Your Word:

"Don't hide your light! Let it shine for all; let your good deeds glow for all to see, so that they will praise your heavenly Father." (Matthew 5:16 The Living Bible).

"You are the light of the world. A city set on a hill cannot be hid." (Matthew 5:14 Revised Standard Version).

"No one lights a lamp and hides it! Instead, he puts it on a lampstand to give light to all who enter the room." (Luke 11:33 The Living Bible).

For I tell you, dear one, your light should not be concealed but is made to shine for others to see—to see Me. For the brighter you shine the brighter am I. Your light cannot be hidden nor can it go out. It is meant to be elevated, on a stand, in order to let others see it. So dear one, let your light shine before men.

Then, Jesus, I desire the courage to shine my light! So give me what I need to fully and completely write this book with joy so my light will shine.

"You're here to be light, bringing out the God-colors in the world."

Matthew 5:14
The Message

Path of Beginnings

The Journey Begins

Lord, I am excited to begin our journey together. You, me, and my journal. You mean everything to me and I want to try and express this love I feel for You in writing.

I put this desire in you, My beloved. I have been waiting for this moment for a long time.

For in the soothing stillness ...
In the peaceful calm ...
In the quiet place ...
There is ...

The Two of Us.

Wonder

My First Encounter with Jesus

I wonder about You God. Who are You? Are You there?

I am here. I have always been here. I know you are curious about Me. I know what you need right now that will guide you to Me. It may not make sense right now but when you think back on this time you will understand. For now, remember what I tell you. Keep it in your heart and don't let go of it. This is what you need to hear, My precious child ...

I am always with you.
I will always protect you.

[I was nine years old when God gave me these promises. As He told me to do, I tucked them away in my heart. Even at age nine, I knew this was from God, the way it made me feel safe and loved. As you will see, these promises from God will be a strong and everlasting thread in my life journey. Much later in my adult life I found these Scriptures:

"... and be sure of this—that I am with you always, even to the end of the world." (Matthew 28:20 The Living Bible).

"The Lord keeps you from all harm and watches over your life." (Psalm 121:7 New Living Translation).]

A Seed of Compassion

I am taking you on a trip with Me, My child. It will be a trip to show you how I have created you. I shaped your heart to love other people. You will start to feel this at a young age as you become drawn towards helping others. This is all you need to know now. The rest will develop beautifully as you grow in love.

I am seeing an image in my mind of us together, Jesus. We are hand in hand flying above the earth, slowly looking down upon Your people. I'm feeling something being planted in my heart. It feels like a desire to love and help other people. A joy is filling my whole being. I see affection on Your face, Jesus, as You hold my hand and show me Your world in need.

God, is this You? Is this us? Somehow I know it is.

This is us, My child. I have planted a seed in your heart for helping others in need. You will see it unfold later in your life. Until then, let it stay there and grow. It will flourish in its right time.

[Ever since this experience with Jesus, I have felt compassion for others and still do. In my 30's, I thought maybe I was to be a missionary because the sense of helping others was so strong. Though no doors seemed to open for this, I held it in my heart. Then something began to happen.

While in my 40's, God made a way for my daughter, Ashley, and me to take a mission trip to Bolivia. It was on this trip that I met three women, Sue, Melodee, and Susie, who have become my dearest of friends. Shortly after this, I began taking short-term mission trips to Oaxaca, Mexico with these friends to help a missionary woman there with her quilting ministry. Being quilters ourselves, we helped her teach the girls and women of the orphanage to quilt, as well as the women and men of the neighboring villages and prisons. This helped enable them to learn a skill and sell what they made.

My heart was full with joy to be doing something I felt was given to me so long ago. To this day, I still hold the seed of compassion in my heart while continuing to help others in need. A true fulfillment of my childhood image—who God created me to be.]

The Embrace

The Embrace

Lord, I love being held in Your arms. There is no other place I would rather be. I feel safe, secure, loved, comfortable, protected, and contented. I feel every bit like a child, snuggled pleasantly in Your arms. Your embrace feels gentle—like a mother's cradle, yet strong—like a father's devotion. I start to relax as I settle into Your tender embrace. I know You won't let me go, for this is our time together and we both are contented. Let me linger here, in Your forever love.

You are precious to Me, My child. I have waited for this embrace. For you to come to Me and want to feel My love for you. I love you so. Even when we are not in this place together, I am embracing you, being your strength and refreshment. I am just a glance or whisper away. I can't get any closer to you than I already am. When you reach out, I am there. I reach out too, for you to take My hand and walk with Me. So, come, My child, anytime, anywhere. I am here.

Father's Embrace

One thing I will ask of You, this will I pray:
To dwell in Your house, O Lord, every day;
To gaze upon Your lovely face,
And rest in the Father's embrace.

~ Stuart Townend, Song Lyrics ~

> ✝
>
> "The eternal God is your refuge, and his everlasting arms are under you."
>
> Deuteronomy 33:27
> New Living Translation

My Desire

My Lord, this feeling in me that draws me to You feels so sweet, pure and secure. I sense it and desire what it holds for me. I am young and do not know of You and all Your ways, though I deeply desire to find them. I find myself reading books that may help me find You. I'm reading Your Word and trying to understand it. For now, I follow Your light where it leads me. Our love for each other is my guide.

I love your desire to be with Me and wanting to know Me more deeply. The more you study and search for Me, the more you will find Me. I am always in the background helping you draw near to Me. Oh, how I love it when you find Me. Your joy fills My heart to such heights. As you continue to mature as a child of Mine, you will start to recognize Me more in your daily life, in the senses of your spirit and My voice in your heart. I speak to you often and My presence is always with you. As you search for Me you will find Me. As you speak to Me I listen and respond. Feel free to respond to Me, My child. I love it when you do.

> "The Lord your God wins victory after victory and is always with you. He celebrates and sings because of you, and he will refresh your life with his love."
>
> Zephaniah 3:17
> Contemporary English Version

Growing Older

Growing Older

Father, as I grow in age and faith, one thread stays sweetly woven—my love of You through journaling. My younger years are passing and I am growing older. I am learning to express myself in deeper ways through writing and I feel You more securely rooted in my heart. How will these next years be with You, Lord? The things I have already learned and experienced have been so inspiring and wonderfully made. What's next for me, Lord? What's next for the two of us?

What wonderful questions, dear one. Let's look into them together. My desire is to explore with you what has been, what is now and what will be. They all tie together. But, do not linger in the past nor worry about the future. The present moment is where I want you to dwell. When you think of the past, look for clues to how I created you to be. When you look at the future, notice your dreams and desires and hold them up to Me for I will make them a reality. Then in the moment at hand, see how they all tie together. For when you were born, you embodied all you were created to be. Then, through life circumstances, much of that faded. Now, it's time to reclaim, reembody who you were created to be. It's all being put together for you, dear one. Are you ready, My child? Adventure awaits!

My First Love

Jesus, You are my first love. I knew this as soon as I felt You stirring in my heart to be Yours. I loved You from the start and nothing has changed. You pursued me when I didn't even know You, yet I knew that You were there, somehow and somewhere. It seems like I've always had a sense of You even when I didn't know You as my Savior. There was an inner knowing of Your love for me and You drawing me close to You. I love that feeling and will never forget it no matter my age. As I grow older, I pray, Lord, our love will grow and grow. I feel so much love for You yet I also feel a longing to give and receive even more. I pray my longing will be answered.

My child, I've known you forever, ever since My first thought of you. You were made in My image. I know everything about you. I love you deeply, tenderly and uniquely. I want you to know this and take it in, just as you breathe. Know I am here, always here. I did pursue you at a young age. I knew you would hear Me and listen to My voice. I've known that all along about you. I knew you would respond to My love freely given to you. Our love for each other will grow and grow. Watch it happen and receive it, like a fountain of life.

The Gift

I am completely overwhelmed by Your goodness right now, Jesus. My tears fill my eyes as I ponder Your kindness towards me. What my heart has longed for has been placed before me. My soul is satisfied. My spirit feels at one with You. My whole being is at peace. It feels as if Your heart and mine are beating together. There is nothing missing. I am complete in You. What I am experiencing is Your great presence. Never let me take Your presence for granted. It is too special. It is You, my Lord. You in all Your glory.

My presence is always with you. Come to Me often and receive My love and peace. We are one. And your soul is satisfied in just being with Me and I with you. What you are experiencing is our unity together as one. This is what you were made for. This is what I want you to feel, again and again. Come often, My dear one, and share in My oneness. It is yours.

In the Beginning

I have been pondering my birth, Lord. I am curious, as if You put that curiosity in me, to ask You when I was actually created. I know that You say in Scripture You knew me before time began, but what does that mean? Lord, what I mean to say is, how far back does Your love go?

I knew you were pondering your birth and I am glad you asked this question. Go back to the beginning, back to the beginning in Genesis. Here you will find your answer and more.

As I open my Bible to the place You directed me to look, my eyes gaze upon the words that make my heart leap. The words are ...

In the beginning ...

Before there was human life, I was known by You. Even when the earth was void, I was on Your mind. In the beginning, I was uniquely designed by You and You knew me. You knew when I was going to be conceived on earth by my parents yet in Your world I had already been known to You.

Yes, for before I formed you in the womb I knew you, and before you were born I set you apart. Just as I created stars, oceans, and land by the words, "Let there be ..." I created you by the words, "Let there be Shelly." I spoke you forth as only a Creator could do.

My dear one, I say to you ... Let there be Shelly!

Father, I can scarcely take this in. I have never heard these words before. You are speaking so deeply within my soul, that so desires to hear this, but would never ask for it. I don't think I even knew how. You are my Creator. You foreknew me, how I would look, how I would act, what I would do in life and everything in between. You knew my name before my parents even chose it. You are my true Father, my Father whom I love with all my heart. I love hearing You say my name. Please don't ever stop. Lord, don't ever stop.

Shelly. What a beautiful name. It brings Me such joy to see how you love hearing it. I will never stop saying your name, dear one. It is My desire to call you by name.

I love being with You, Jesus, and learning from You. I feel You speaking to my heart. When I pause to consider the sensation of You speaking to my heart, I can but only strive to put it in words. I sense Your presence descend on me with a gentle embrace of my whole being, getting my attention to stop and take notice. I feel enveloped by You in an unearthly way I don't experience at any other time. In what feels like seconds, my heart interprets in words what You are saying to me. I feel loved, cherished and held by You. You remain with me for a time and I don't want You to let go. The sensation fades and all I can do is linger in the moment. Anything else would seem incomplete. I don't want the feeling to end. I have never felt such love. I love You, my Lord. From in the beginning ...

"I have set the Lord always before me …"

Psalm 16:8
English Standard Version

Behold Me Beholding You

Jesus, I tenderly feel Your presence. The soft movement in and around me makes me smile and look towards what I can sense in front of me. It is You before me. I begin to reach out my hand, not to offer mine, but to receive Yours already extended toward me. I place my hand in Yours as it seems to rest perfectly. I can scarcely contain my joy as I continue to smile and look upward. Then, You speak to me ...

Look at My face. My eyes. My gaze.

In my mind's image of You I see Your face. Your eyes. Your gaze. Then You speak to me again ...

My child, you become what you behold.
Now, behold Me beholding you.

All I can do to respond is to rest in this moment and say, as slight breath spills from my lips ...

My beloved, I tenderly rest in wonder at the gaze of Your love towards me.

Behold Our God

Who has held the oceans in His hands?
Who has numbered every grain of sand?
Kings and nations tremble at His voice
All creation rises to rejoice

Behold our God seated on His throne
Come, let us adore Him
Behold our King! Nothing can compare
Come, let us adore Him!

~ Jonathon Baird, Meghan Baird, Ryan Baird,
Stephen Altrogge, Song Lyrics ~

Lord, Prepare My Heart to Praise You

I am so excited to begin my time with You in worship. Help me to enter Your courts with praise. Help me to focus on who You are and what You are like as my God, as my Savior and as my Holy Spirit, fully alive in my life. I desire to express myself as fully and freely as I know how to do. Guide me, Holy Spirit. Teach me, Lord. As I love You through my worship of You.

You are so loving towards Me, My child. So willing to free yourself up to be with Me and express your love towards Me. Yes, I will guide you and teach you as you worship. And remember, the heavens are worshiping too.

Praise

†

When I think of loving You, God, through praise, I wonder what it will be like as I celebrate my way to deeper awareness of my connection with You.

Heart Praises

I Love Your Praises

Sometimes, Father, I can't seem to express all that's inside of me that wants to praise You. It's such yearning that comes from a deep place within me and at this moment seems to be never ending or without desire. Praising You is how I want to live and breathe. It's what I want to do all day as I cry out to You …

I love You, Lord! You are worthy to be praised!

I want you to know, My beloved, that I love your praises. In fact, I remember each one. I hold them in My heart and know the place of love from which they were said to Me. Speak them to Me. Sing them to Me. Dance them to Me. With all that you are and all that you have, keep praising Me. I love you, dear one. And I am delighting in your praises right now.

Praise You from Your Word

I have always been captivated by Your Word, Lord. It connects Your truth to something deep inside of me that fills me with joy and makes me want to praise You. Your Word feels alive to me, pops off the pages as it speaks about how it was meant just for me. It helps me think of things I haven't thought of before and helps me with situations in my life. Most of all, Your Word makes me fall in love with You all over again and again. Your Word ignites praise in me for You!

"From the rising of the sun to the place where it sets, the name of the Lord is to be praised." (Psalm 113:3 New International Version).

"Let me live that I may praise you ..." (Psalm 119:175 New International Version).

"My soul yearns, even faints, for the courts of the Lord; my heart and my flesh cry out for the living God." (Psalm 84:2 New International Version).

"With all my heart I will praise you." (Psalm 86:12 The Living Bible).

"I will praise the Lord God with a song and a thankful heart." (Psalm 69:30 Contemporary English Version).

"You have rescued me! I will celebrate and shout, singing praises to you with all my heart." (Psalm 71:23 Contemporary English Version).

"With all my heart I praise the Lord, and with all that I am I praise his holy name! With all my heart I praise the Lord! I will never forget how kind he has been." (Psalm 103:1-2 Contemporary English Version).

"I will praise the Lord at all times; his praise is always on my lips. My whole being praises the Lord." (Psalm 34:1-2 The Expanded Bible).

"Give praise to the Lord, proclaim his name; make known among the nations what he has done, and proclaim that his name is exalted." (Isaiah 12:4 New International Version).

"The trumpeters and musicians joined in unison to give praise and thanks to the Lord. Accompanied by trumpets, cymbals and other instruments, the singers raised their voices in praise to the Lord and sang: "He is good; his love endures forever." (2 Chronicles 5:13 New International Version).

I love your praises, My child. I love the way they make you so joyful and exuberant. You make Me sing too!

Beautiful Creation

Precious Lord, I'm ready for a wonderful day filled with You in it!

Father, what beauty is in Your creation. In an instant, I feel connected to You in a way that feels unworldly, yet near me presently. For You have created this morning in hopes that I will take notice of Your artistry. My eyes behold Your delightful creation and my soul breathes in Your goodness. The mountains in the distance are grand. The flowers of all kinds are in full bloom. The sky is a perfect shade of blue with fluffy white clouds slowly sweeping across. There is a warm breeze blowing through the thick leaved trees nearby my house, and it's all accompanied by the songs of You, Lord. Thank You for being nothing less than who You are—for being You. You are magnificent in every way and I am filled with excitement to be here with You, in Your beautiful creation!

Take your time. Take it all in. I created nature for you to enjoy. You could look all around this earth and still not see all that is here for you to savor. When you notice something that captures your heart, pause, look at it once, twice, and again until your heart is full. Then you will have met Me there in that moment. I love when you take the time to pause and notice. It's a moment when we can meet and spend time together. I love spending time with you, My dear one.

Melody of Delight

I remember a recent time when I was praising You with the humming of a song I was making up on my own. I was joyfully humming away and enjoying what was being created. "This is for You, Lord!" I thought. A smile even broke over my face as I carried on and on. Then a lovely image came to my mind. It was of You listening to me humming my song and putting it to music. Beautiful orchestral music filled my ears. So lovely. Then I noticed that You were the conductor of the orchestra. The look on Your face was of pure delight. Delight in my song reaching Your ears and then having the orchestra play it so it could reach my ears. Oh, the music we were playing together!

I am listening to you intently, My dear one, and with great joy and enchantment. You are making up such a delightful song of praise to Me. Oh, how I love your praise! It's all I can do but give it back to you through music I know speaks to your heart. You see, dear one, I love to bless you too!

Room for Praise

Father, there is always room, ways and means to praise You. There is an eternity to the ways You can be praised. And someday I will spend my eternity praising You face to face. When I find myself in the darkest places, I know You are there with me because Your love for me was there first. You don't want me to be alone. You join me in my struggles and walk alongside me. Your light shines and guides me. Even if it's just a tiny glow, it will never go out. That, my God, is worthy of praise.

I find joy in your praises, dear one. I never get tired of hearing them. They bring joyous melodies to My heavens which echo spontaneous exultation before My throne. You never know what your praises will do for those who hear them. There is always room and more room for praise.

Praise You for Your Character

Father, when I think of praising You I think of Your character and who You are to me. That brings about much in my mind regarding Your greatness and goodness. There are endless ways to name Your praises. Countless ways to express how I feel, yet never feeling like I've exhausted the list. That is why Your praises endure forever! I love You, dearest Lord, and here is why.

Father, You are faithful and true to Your Word. Your faithfulness is everlasting!

I praise You for being perfect in all Your ways. You are unmatched!

I praise You for Your unfailing and constant love. Your love is from everlasting to everlasting!

Is there any limit to Your goodness and kindness? For Your limitlessness I praise Thee!

I praise You for Your Kingship on Your majestic throne of grace. You reign in victory!

Father, I praise You for Your unmatched power. None can compare!

I praise You for Your vastness. You cannot be contained!

Father, You are slow to anger and abounding in love. Praise You for being so patient and bountiful in Your love for me!

I praise You for being my fierce protector. You hem me in from all sides!

You are a loving father and a tender mother. You know when I need each!

I praise You for Your light that leads my path. You brightly illuminate my way in good times and bad!

I praise You for Your creation. Made for all to see and enjoy!

Father, You are a fountain of life. You spring forth living water!

I praise You that You are the King of Kings. Your Lordship reigns forever!

I praise You for being a Wonderful Counselor. My Advocate for life!

I praise You for being a Prince of Peace. You are calming through storms!

Father, I praise You for being Mighty to save. Salvation is Your name!

I praise You for Your character that never changes. You are forever good!

I praise You for being a friend that never turns His back. My best friend!

I praise You for being a constant provider. You are just in time with what is best for me!

I praise You for being the Bread of Life. He who comes to You will never go hungry!

Father, You are the Good Shepherd. You keep me and lead me as Your sheep!

I praise You for being the Resurrection and the Life. All who live in You will never die!

I feel how much praise I have for You now on this earth and I burst knowing what praise will be like in heaven!

Praising You, Lord, comes from my heart because You are in my heart. Every beat is for You and because of You!

I pray that no matter what happens I can still have breath to praise You and love You!

Shouting, "Praise God!" doesn't begin to describe how I feel. When I get to heaven will I know then the words I can't find now?

I give You the highest praise, Father. You deserve this no matter what my life is like.

With all my heart, I praise Thee!

Oh, My dear one, how I love your praises! Know that they reach the heavens, to My very ears. I celebrate with you for I know what it is to live amongst praise. Never cease to worship. I'll never cease to receive. I love you, dear one. Always, I love you.

Praise You from My Heart

Father, I love when You and I can share moments from daily life together that are so meaningful to my soul. Each one I write down in my journal.

I love Your beauty, Lord. Your face is lovely and Your gaze is mine. I love beholding You.

If You did nothing else for me today, Lord, then just spend time with me right now, I would know the depths of Your love for me.

It is with You, Lord, that I know I am loved. Even one brief moment in Your presence tells my soul, "Shelly, you are dearly cherished." Father, You have my entire heart.

Sweet Lord, I am touched by the ways You capture my heart with Your love. You beckon my whole heart to be with Yours. Father, I am Yours.

May my lips ever flow with praise for You, Jesus. You are always worthy of praise. May I never get tired or complacent about my feelings toward You. It is because of Your great mercy and grace I have the life I have. You are my King and are so worthy of my praise.

Dear one, I love what flows from your heart, My living water springs forth from within you.

Praise You for This Day

Every morning starts a new day with You, Jesus. I love telling you how I feel about it in my journal.

Good morning, sweet Jesus! What a wonderful day is ahead. Lord, let me be ready and responsive to all You have to offer and let me be cheerful and willing in giving back to others.

What a glorious day full of discovery and adventure. There is so much to learn about You and so much I don't know but am anxious to find out. I am full of excitement for a new door has opened in my life and I am experiencing some wonderful things.

Father, it's a wonderful day already just because You are in it.

Today, is a beautiful day. The birds are singing delightful melodies. You are in every note.

Wonderful God full of abundant love and grace, oh, how I love You. I love You and love to spend time with You. You are my shelter where I feel comfortable and safe, relaxed and loved. I know You are with me no matter what. You are my great love.

It's a new year, Lord. Only time has changed, You are still the same. You are beyond my comprehension, yet, what I do understand, I love and seek.

I am so excited about spending time with You today and every day. You are the one person I can spend hours with. Being in Your presence for even a moment fills my soul for a lifetime.

What wonderful opportunities will spill forth today, Lord?

Lord, it is a beautiful morning of uninterrupted time with You. No schedule constraints, just peaceful and quiet moments together with You. Even in my anxiousness You are calming and easing, relaxing and gentle. I can feel Your hand upon me and can feel myself slowing down and knowing I'm entering a holy place and holy time.

I have a lot of thoughts going through my mind about what I am going to do today. But the first thing I want to do is tell You, "I love You."

I love that you have joy and appreciation for each day. Your curiosity and wonder are wonderful ways to approach your days. This will serve you well throughout your life. Remember Me every time you feel this beautiful expression of emotion overflowing. You are wonderfully made, My child.

Lord, Prepare My Heart for Prayer

I think about my thoughts toward You regarding going further into my heart of prayer, Lord. I know it can only help me to continue preparing my heart for what's ahead. Writing them down helps me understand you more.

I see You in all things. Even when I don't have the strength or courage to reach out to You, I see You and I love You. I want You to know that, Lord.

There is no direction I'd rather go than towards You.

I desire to stay close to You. Anywhere else is too far away.

God, You are wonderful, glorious, and majestic. You fill me with joy beyond my comprehension. It's a feeling that's hard to put into words so help me put it into action.

You make the world's issues surmountable because You guide me step by step.

You are everything I want to be, Oh, Lord.

I'm glad we are friends, Jesus.

Your love turned my heart inside out. If You had not, I would not know the love I was missing.

Lord, You bless me so much. How can I bless You?

Dear one, how I love your thoughts towards Me. They are sweet to My ears. I feel your excitement for life, for My creation and your love for Me. Nothing is more lovely than the expression of your love for Me. You have My attention and My devotion. Whatever your thoughts are I want to hear them. It's My joy to spend time with you no matter when or for how long. It's knowing that you love Me that delights Me. All this blesses Me. Your heart is prepared. Know that all this you have said, is prayer. All that you have gone through and will go through is prayer.

†

"Rose early to seek God and found Him whom my soul loveth. Who would not rise early to meet such company?"

~ Robert Murray M'Cheyne ~

Prayer

†

When I think of prayer, Father,
I ponder how my senses awaken to
the One I am in love with.

Secret Place of Prayer

I enjoy praying the most when I'm alone with You, Jesus, just the two of us. I can be truly who I am and You show me who You truly are. I savor both. Certain Scriptures have held the truth of this secret time with You, Lord.

"When you pray, go to your room and close the door. Pray privately to your Father who is with you. Your Father sees what you do in private. He will reward you." (Matthew 6:6 God's Word Translation).

"In the morning, long before sunrise, Jesus went to a place where he could be alone to pray." (Mark 1:35 God's Word Translation).

My heart has always felt more alive with You when we are alone together in quiet places, especially nature, with no one around. It is our secret place. It is where Your presence is felt and Your voice is heard the most. I feel and hear you throughout my day as well, but our secret place of prayer is my sacred place with You. That is why I spend so much time there, Father. It started that way from the beginning and will always be. Thank You for our quiet places together, Jesus.

I created you, dear one to hear My voice and feel My presence. I made you to crave sacred space this way not only to be with Me, but to develop your voice, your own unique voice that would tell of Me. So keep journaling. I am training your voice. Training your light to shine.

The Stillness

The quiet fills my soul. It is my friend. Always has been. It is the stillness which speaks to me. The more I am in contemplation, the more I talk to You and the more I hear You talking to me. I am also aware of Your presence, Lord. It is that familiarity of You that I seek.

Dear one, there is movement in the stillness. It's flowing, refreshing, soothing, calming, and life-giving. It's a gentle stirring. Give into it. For it is Me, Your Father. In the silence, you see, hear, and feel the movement. It is Me, Your Holy Spirit.

Be open to the arrival of moments and movements. Every moment that is was already created in the beginning. When one passes, there is another which follows. They are always there. So, relax in the arrival of moments. I am in them to be found.

Be still and know that I am God. I am with you. In the eternity of moments, I am with you, dear one. Be still.

It's Enough

I am so excited about being here with You in prayer. As I sit quietly, I'm beginning to relax and smile as we draw closer together. What will it be like, Jesus? The more I relax and wonder, the more I feel Your presence moving in me. The more I am around You the more I want to be around You.

What should we do first, Lord?

What should we talk about, Lord?

I can feel You smiling at me. You know I can't help but smile back.

I am smiling at you, Shelly.

And that, Lord, is what I need.

"Prayer is the nearest approach to God and the highest enjoyment of Him that we are capable of in life."

~ William Law ~

Prayer Steps

Jesus, taking this walk with You is so comforting and relaxing. I love the path we are on, lined with prairie grass on both sides. I love prairie fields. They are the perfect height. That way I can see over them onto all the blooming flowers mixed in. I love the way they blow in the breeze in rhythm, almost orchestrating a song.

I'm contemplating what the next step is going to be in my prayer life. I am trying new things in regards to praying for others. I'm used to praying out loud or in my head for people. But I'm feeling Your encouragement to try holding them in my heart where Your love resides so I can pray for them throughout the day. That feels good to me. Something I would like to try. As I write their names and requests down in my journal, I will also tuck them away in the love of my heart. This feels like my next step in learning about praying for others.

I am glad we are on this walk together. I knew you would enjoy the prairie fields! I did place this new idea in your heart to consider praying for others in a new way. It is good to try new ways of intercession. All prayer comes straight to My ears and heart. And I love the sound of it no matter if it comes through words, silence or in your heart. It all matters to Me and to the person you are praying for.

Get ready for my heart prayers then, Father!

Where You Lead Me

I find myself sitting on a bench again with You in a forest, a place I love to be with You. I want to talk to You about where You are leading me next in my prayer life. You shepherd me in so many beautiful ways that help guide me spiritually and make my love for You even stronger. Though I'm excited about where You may be leading me, I have a fear to tell You. I know in my head it is irrational, but somehow it still worries me. I don't know where You are taking me, Lord. Will this new leading in my life take me somewhere where I won't be able to hear Your voice? Being in Your presence and hearing Your voice are what I love about our relationship. I know there are times when You are silent, and I experience those times. But for some reason, at this time, my heart is concerned. I want You to know how I feel. I want to place my heart in Your hands, the hands I trust.

Never worry about what you are thinking or want to express to Me. You can bring anything to Me and I am here to listen. My hands are open and holding your worries and fears. You can trust Me. You can always trust Me. And even when you have a hard time, I will still be with you. Always with you. I know I am leading you to a different place in your prayer life. But remember this, I will never lead you away from My voice. My sheep hear My voice.

Lord, I can't tell You how much that means to me. To know that no matter where I am in life, I can never be away from Your beautiful voice and presence. I know that in my mind, though I often forget, but now I feel it in my heart, in that deep place where truth lies. I feel better now.

I am always here when you need Me, My dear one. You can trust Me. You can trust Me with your whole heart. If not all at first, share with Me the parts you can.

☦

"There is not in the world a kind of life more sweet and delightful, than that of a continual conversation with God."

~ Brother Lawrence ~

Safety in Prayer

P rayer is when You see me for who I really am and I see You for who You really are. Both are huge revelations.

Lord, I love what happens between us when we are together in prayer. Sometimes my heart starts out cocooned, not knowing exactly what to say or if I should say it. Sometimes it can be hard to start sharing. Then You meet me in my hesitation. You tell me it's safe and good to share my heart, no matter what it is. Then, slowly my heart starts to open, wanting to peep out. I feel Your safety and I start to put words to what's in my heart.

I am here, dear one. I want to hear your prayers. I know that sometimes it takes time to share your heart and get through all the internal components of your soul. That's okay, dear one. Sometimes, that's how it is supposed to be. For there is a reason for the process. It is designed for self-revelations prompted by your own mind and by Me. This takes time on your part—to let the noise and anxiousness start to settle out of your mind. Then the real work can be done. This is where the two of us meet.

I feel safe, Lord.

Acceptance

P rayer helps me unearth my unique relationship with You. When I talk to You with words or in silence, it is how we get to know each other. My relationship with You, God, means more to me than just talking to You. It's when I come to You to be held in Your arms and they are already open. It's when I need a hug and I hear Your voice say, "You are loved." It's when I go to You, Jesus, because I feel out of control. Then I begin to relax when You gently remind me that You are in control. It's when I need to cry on the shoulder of my Savior, and I start to feel Your tears covering mine. It's a place I go when I feel like no one else will accept me. I begin to feel You as my refuge as You whisper to me, "I accept you."

You can come to Me with all your feelings and all your thoughts. You are always accepted. I will be there with open arms. My arms are always waiting for you.

One in Prayer

One in Prayer

Father, in Your presence is where I need to be right now. That place in Your heart where You hold Your prayers is where I want to be with mine. I have many. I can't imagine how many You keep safe. My heart's desire is to align with Your heart. You know who I am praying for and what they need. Help me know this so I can pray more precisely.

My heart is full with My love for who I have created. I hear all prayers. I know them before they are even spoken. Prayers bring joy to My heart because they are coming from the very lips of My loved ones. Prayers also bring tears as I know the pain My loved ones hold. No matter what the prayers, no matter how often they are spoken, I receive them all, forever. For you, My dear one, My heart holds the words you seek in order for you to know what I feel for My loved ones. It is good that you seek this. Yet, also know, I love to hear what's in your own heart. And then there are those moments when both of our hearts come together in a single prayer of alignment. Our words become one. It is beautiful.

You give me so much to think about. When I'm with You there is clarity and understanding even when I come in with confusion or questions. You have helped me understand more about prayer and how You see it. I feel You so much right now that it's taking my breath away yet at the same time I feel full of breath. I love You so much, Father.

The Lake

I need to sit with You by the lake today, God. It's where I need to be and I want it to be with You, my sweet Lord. I feel overwhelmed with life right now. I can feel it in my shoulders and neck. I want to just sink into this chair with deep breaths to calm me. As I breathe, sitting still, I look at the lake and my whole body starts to settle down. I notice the vastness of the water and hear the waves on the surface, gently gliding onto the rock shore. I feel tranquil. I could sit here all day when I feel like this. I close my eyes and feel the breeze on my face and the smell of a fresh day. I start to feel Your presence, Lord. It gently starts to wash over me until I am completely enveloped by You.

With Your sweet presence surrounding me I open my eyes and see the water again and feel so harmoniously connected to You, creation, and life. It's as if I am one with You. All the worries and stress I came with just peel away and seem to disappear. Even if it's just for this one moment, I am truly content. I love You, Lord. I love You.

My dear one, I find great joy when you are aware of My presence. It's how I live and I always want to share it with you. Telling Me how content you are just being with Me tells Me My work on the cross has met you in this moment. For, I sent the Holy Spirit to be with you and live inside you always. You can never be any closer to Me than that. I love you, dear one. I love you.

Joy

I feel such a joy when I am in prayer with You that I don't want our time together to end. But when it does, I know we leave together. Our joy remains with us.

Yet, sometimes, it seems to fade as times get difficult. Your presence is constant, yet sometimes it feels like Your joy comes and goes. I know life isn't easy and is not always sunny, but this I know and have experienced—You are joy magnified. I can sense You wanting me to know that joy is within me and around me as a gift ready to be noticed and enjoyed. When I come to You, no matter how I am feeling, You leave me with peace and joy. That's just one more reason I love coming to You!

Beloved, I am always with you no matter where you are or where you go. No matter if you are feeling up or down. I love that you shared your heart, so honestly, about your joy being fleeting sometimes. Joy is a gift from Me that I have placed in your heart as a way to notice and celebrate Me and all I have created. It's a love sign pointing to all that is to be praised and delighted in. It brings to full circle the jubilation of you, Me, creation, and others. I love when you feel joy in My presence. Take your joy with you wherever you go. Others will benefit from your outpouring, for joy is increased by spreading it to others.

My Ears, My Eyes

If I would just use the eyes and ears You gave me, Lord, instead of the ones I made for myself, I could see and hear You all over the place.

Opening yourself up to Me more and more creates new ears to hear and wider eyes to see. Take joy in what you see and hear, My loved one, for I am bigger than you can know. Pray for you to know Me, even more beyond your own understanding and knowledge of Me. Pray for My greatness to be a larger part of your life. You will not regret it, My child. You will be astounded by what you see and hear.

I do want to know more of Your greatness, Lord. Show me. I do want to know more of You in all things, Jesus. Teach me. Increase my sight. Increase my hearing, I pray.

Unbelief Turns to Faith

O Lord, help me with the words to pray for my friend. For I fear I have none.

Pray these prayers for your friend's salvation. Pray for her to see Me, not as she sees Me now—for that is distorted by her unbelief—but for who I really am. Then she will start to notice Me and feel her unbelief start to melt into the beginnings of faith. This is what I love most.

Oh, yes, Lord. That touches my heart so deeply and coincides with what is good to pray for my friend. I feel it deeply. I can sense You, Holy Spirit, inspiring me to say, in my own words, what You want me to say. My prayers feel strong and effective, powerful and life-giving. Thank You, Father.

That is the work of the Holy Spirit in you. I rise in you to give you the words to say. Words that were deep in your heart but you could not find them. They were also deep in My heart at the same moment. That is true conversation, My child. That is true prayer.

Rescuing

Lord, I need rescuing. My prayer has been, "God, please rescue me."

Perhaps your prayer should be, "God, humble me so I can allow myself to be rescued."

That is such a different way for me to look at it, Lord. It identifies something in me that may need to bow down before You—something that needs to be humbled in me. Help me think about that, Lord. Help me see if there is anything in me that is not right with You.

Your prayer is right where it needs to be. Look inside yourself and reflect upon your own need for humbleness. Your reflection is meant to be soft and gentle, not harsh or self-judging. It's about noticing yourself and what is going on inside of you that's important. Bring those things to Me in prayer so we can talk about them and I can show you how to care for them, how to care for your soul, My daughter.

I'm discovering that I do have some pride issues that need attending to. What leads me to this discovery is when I open my heart up for Your observation. This leads to a compassionate conviction of my heart's plight. It hits a right chord in my mind and spirit. This leads to wanting to admit it to You and then wanting to change my direction.

That is it. You discovered what I was hoping you would. Remember, pride is not acknowledging your sin, unfaithfulness, or wrongdoing, which can lead to being indifferent toward Me in admitting them. Your heart, My daughter, has melted which makes your heart like clay, pliable, workable, and willing.

I am amazed at how much You draw out of me during prayer, Jesus.

It is My love that draws out your uniqueness in prayer. You have a voice that I love to hear. You have emotions that move Me. You have thoughts and feelings that I want you to express. All these things add up to your voice in prayer. The more you practice expressing these essential parts of prayer, the more comfortable and honest you become in My presence.

I love that, Lord. I love feeling more and more comfortable in Your presence. I know it will lead to greater depths into both of our hearts. I love that thought!

In Need of a Savior

Jesus, I need a friend today—a companion to help me understand something hurting my heart. Lord, there is a person I have been praying for who needs You as her Savior. I want her to know You and give her heart to You. I hear Your voice gently speak to me.

Place your heart amid your prayer. I want you to feel what I feel in your request.

I will try, Lord. Instead of just praying words to You, my heart wants to share with You my true emotions, my anger, frustrations, sadness, and doubt. I know You will understand my heart. And at the same time, I want to understand Yours. As I begin to just sit with You and think about my friend, I begin to feel emotions about her life without You. I feel sad and distressed. I know what my life was like without You and what it is like with You now. I can't imagine a life without You for anyone else. I am crying now, Lord. I wonder how You must feel.

Continue to pray to Me, dear one. I want you to express your full emotions from your heart. No words are necessary. Sometimes your heart speaks more to Me. I am sad too. My heart yearns for My own to come to Me. As I wait for her to come to Me, your prayers mean so much. It brings our hearts together in love.

Thank You, Jesus. It does feel like my prayers are bringing our hearts together. This makes me cry more, not tears of sadness but of joy. It feels so good to share my pain with You. It is slowly turning to joy.

I don't know why my friend is not out of the darkness and in Your light, but I do know the depths of Your love for her.

Your friend is My child and I wait patiently until she is Mine.

I trust You, Lord. I wait patiently too. Then, we will celebrate.

Lord, Prepare My Heart for Confession

Father, as I move even deeper into prayer with You, help me prepare my heart to look inward at my own transgressions.

Yes, My child, you are moving ever deeper into prayer and My heart. There you will find things that could never have been found if you weren't willing to take this journey inward. As your heart prepares, know that I will help you discover your iniquities. It is necessary for them to come forth for your own personal growth. Go now, My child, to My cross and surrender yourself to Me.

Confession

†

Lord, when I think of confession, I realize that praise is how I express my love for You ... confession is how You express Your love for me ... through Your forgiveness. Beautiful.

My Offering

Ointment Poured Forth

"Is thy soul sore from sin, from chafing, or from the fiery darts of Satan, of sinners, or of saints? Then is thy Lord to thee as "OINTMENT POURED FORTH," free, abundant, ready, healing and fragrant. Suffering soul, come near to Him and let that healing OINTMENT pour over thee and soothe and heal thee."

~ Charles E. Hurlburt and T.C. Horton ~

As I Acknowledge My Sins, Oh, How You Love Me, God

Sometimes, all I need is to just name and write out my sins. It is soothing to my soul to know that as I write them down, You are receiving them and forgiving me. Thank You, heavenly Father.

I admit that being honest with You, Lord, is the best type of prayer. Then I can accept Your honesty.

I admit that right now I am weak in faith and heavily worried. Help me bring this to You with honesty and a willingness to be changed. For I know that is both of our desires.

Please, Lord, don't let me turn a blind eye to the truth of my own sins. Today, I admit I need to keep admitting. And tomorrow too.

I admit that lately my mind has been more in the earthly world than the spiritual world. Help me to see deeper into Your world, Lord.

My flesh seems weak but my heart is true to You, God.

I have fallen once again. If I let myself be taken away from You every time I feel unworthy, I would never come to You at all. I shall come to You in the good times and the bad.

I expose my heart to You, God, not so You can see it, but so I can see it. You already know it, Lord.

With kindness and forgiveness, I receive your sins. I remember them no more. Now you remember them no more.

Tell me again of how You forgive me, Lord.

As far as the east is from the west. That's how far I have removed your transgressions from you.

Help me feel that, Lord. I want my heart, mind, soul, and strength to feel it.

Your heart is free. Feel My forgiveness. Feel My tenderness and generous love towards you that can never stop, no matter what you do or say. You can't hurt Me. You can't break Me. Your sin has already been taken upon Me at the cross. My work is complete. When you admit your sins and receive My forgiveness with an accepting heart, your work is done.

I receive, Lord. I receive.

The Wound of Sin

I desire to have an honest prayer time before You today. I want to talk about my disappointment in myself over my sins. In my tears and pain I cry out,

Will you forgive me again and again and again for the same sin?

God, you give me an honest answer in the form of a narrow and shaded image. I am seeing a wound up close. It looks like a piece of flesh, freshly scarred. And it looks like it has been wounded so many times that it is red, bleeding, and exposed. It is a picture of Your wound, my Savior, from the sins of the world. You are showing this to me because of the work done on the cross and the forgiveness of sins, once and for all. Though I sin over and over again, and Your forgiveness is constant, I still need a Savior. I feel gently convicted of my sins in a way that brings me into Your presence to talk them through.

Jesus, I am weeping with You over my sins. I feel a sensation within me that seems to clean my insides where sin has been rotting. Jesus, You are taking my burdens away, again. Your forgiveness is forever.

I am finding comfort in Scripture. It speaks to me about sin.

"Out of the depths I cry to you, Lord; Lord, hear my voice. Let your ears be attentive to my cry for mercy. If you, Lord, kept a record of sins, Lord, who could stand? But with you there is forgiveness, so that we can, with reverence, serve you. I wait for the Lord, my whole being waits, and in his word I put my hope." (Psalm 130:1-5 New International Version).

My sins are too much for me to bear. I feel their torment. Help me find relief. Jesus, I feel Your presence. I feel You looking into my eyes. You take my hands in Yours and hold them gently. Not one word is spoken. Your eyes tell the story.

You are forgiven, again and again and again. You are free.

Better Than Thanks Sometimes

As I am spending time with You, Father, it reminds me of how I can come to You with my sins and distresses in my heart and how You hear them so differently than I would hear them myself. You treat me not as my sins deserve but instead with forgiveness and a kiss on my cheek. Sometimes, that love freely given can be better than when I come to You in times of thanksgiving or praise.

I am beholding you, My child. You are so dear to Me. So precious. My mercies are grace kisses upon your cheek. Receive them. They are made especially for you. New every morning. I love you, My child.

Heart of Forgiveness

Please God, forgive me of my sins. Those which are known to me and those which are unknown to me. Sometimes I feel as though I haven't fully surrendered everything to You even though I think I have. Why is that, Lord?

As I sit with You more in silence, I begin to feel something happen to me inwardly. I recognize that feeling. It's Your presence. So lovely. So sweet. I don't want this moment to end. Your presence lingers and so do I. Then without any effort on my part, I notice a gentle awakening of knowledge coming over me. Lightly, it starts to flow as it begins to become alive in me. It seems to linger as I try and capture what is happening between us. What You share with me in my heart is beautiful.

I love that we are here together sharing this moment. When you come to Me with an asking heart for forgiveness, it is freely given. For this is why I died for you. Your sins are already forgiven. Asking Me for forgiveness is for your own heart to know your weaknesses and begin to turn them into strengths. Search your heart again. Listen deeply. I am revealing things to you that you need to know to understand things beyond where you have searched in your heart. They aren't so deep that they are out of your reach. A listening posture and openness to receive is all you need.

As you do this, your heart will soften more and more. Your mind will relax from its constant meandering. Then, it comes to you, held by My love, the realization that you haven't fully surrendered your sins to Me. As we spend this time together, they are becoming known to you, gently and truthfully. No judgement, just a revealing that opens a whole new world of understanding of your own sin, even ones you were not aware of. My love is holding them in the light of compassion. Now, My beloved, ask Me again. Ask Me for forgiveness.

Savior, will You forgive me?

I died for this moment, My child. I died for the forgiveness of sins. Therefore, walk, My daughter, walk in forgiveness. Walk in freedom. I died for your freedom. Live in victory.

God's Gaze

Father, I know sin is the biggest barrier that keeps me from You. All I want to do is be with You and all I feel is shame which keeps me from You. Why is this so hard? Why can't it go away? I'm not going to let it be a wedge between us. I feel unworthy to be in Your presence but I can't turn and walk away either.

My child, come to Me as you are, no matter how you feel about yourself. I will show you how much I love you and how much you matter to Me. Close your eyes and look at Me. Look at My face gazing upon you. Can you feel My gaze? It is a gaze of love and not shame. You are an image of Me. Take on My image of love without shame. Look at yourself now, My child.

I'm sitting in my favorite chair with my eyes closed wanting to experience You, Jesus. I am desperate for Your love to take away my shame, even a little. I don't care how long it takes, just meet me here, Jesus. A slight warmth is starting to come over me. Almost instantly, I can feel myself smiling even with a slight laugh. A soothing awareness comes over me like a blanket. I feel Your love, Lord. There is no disapproval or judgement, just Your love in me and all around me. Oh, Lord, yes, yes, I can feel Your gaze! Your eyes speak of forgiveness without shame. I receive Your shameless love!

That is how much I love you. That I showed My great love for you by sending My Son to die for you while you were still a sinner. This is the gaze of love I have upon you. Every time you see yourself, remember Me.

Sin Is Not My Friend

Sin is not my friend even though it tries to act like it. Satan's voice tries to lure me, tempt me, and trick me into thinking things that are not true about me, my life, others and You, Lord. Sometimes, when I hear this trickery, I start to believe it. Then I start to play that message over and over in my mind until I might act upon it or maybe I start to make it part of my belief system.

Then there are times when, even in the middle of the recording in my head, something interrupts my thought process and I start to hear truth up against those lies. Eventually, the truth becomes louder than the lies and I take great notice. Lord, You would never lie to me or confuse me. I am choosing to believe Your truth over Satan's lies. Help me now to be strong-minded towards Your truths and resistant to the lies. In this moment, I draw near to truth, Your truth. I pray Satan would stop placing his thoughts on top of Yours, Oh, Lord. I draw near and I feel Satan departing.

You are a conqueror and are showing great strength in this moment. This will help you in future moments when Satan tries to snare you again. As you draw near to Me, the devil will flee from you. This is My promise.

The Cross

Lord, I love being on this retreat with You. Being in nature and spending unlimited time with You fills my soul to overflowing. Today, I feel drawn to Your cross. I first noticed a cross in the sanctuary where I spent some time contemplating Your suffering for me. Then, outside in the garden, was a statue of You on the cross. It was there that I contemplated my sins against You. When I went back inside the retreat building, I noticed a cross on the wall. As I begin to stop and look closely, I notice something that surprises me. It has a mirror at the center. When I thought I was looking at You, I was actually looking at myself. At first, Lord, I don't want to look at myself but as I allow myself to look, something changes. It is as if I am looking at You as well as me. I see Your reflection in me.

There is much to learn at the foot of My cross. When you ponder My suffering in light of your sins, a transformation begins to happen. You begin to understand that I created you and died for you for the same reason. So that you may live. It is good to see Me at the cross. Don't be afraid to look in the mirror. See. Reflect. Live out what you see in the mirror.

†

"For every look at self, take ten looks at Christ."

~ Robert Murray M'Cheyne ~

Come, Thou Fount of Every Blessing

Oh, to grace how great a debtor
Daily I'm constrained to be
Let Thy goodness, like a fetter
Bind my wandering heart to Thee
Prone to wander, Lord, I feel it
Prone to leave the God I love
Here's my heart, oh, take and seal it
Seal it for Thy courts above

~ Robert Robinson, Song Lyrics ~

New Mercies

God, you have given me new mercies today. You want to be with me even though I am someone who has forgotten about being with You.

My mercies are made new every day. They are always waiting for you no matter why you need them. And with My mercies is My forever love.

Thank You, Lord. When I hear You say this to me it makes me want to curl up in Your arms and be held. Hold me, Lord. Please, hold me.

Receive My open arms, My child, for as long as you need them. They are yours forever.

Lord, Prepare My Heart for Struggles

This is a hard one, Lord. Hard because I must go beyond searching my heart to discover my sins and admitting them. I have to go now to that deep place of pain and sorrow over the things in my life that bring me sadness.

This is hard for Me too because I don't like to see you in pain or discomfort. Yet, I know it is part of being human. I too experienced pain and sorrow and got through it by leaning on My Father. This is what I ask of you as you continue to enter this deep part of your soul. I am tender towards your wounds and will care for them as I care for every part of you. Enter in, My dear one. You won't be sorry and you may be surprised by the outcome.

Struggles

†

When I think of my struggles, I recognize that the times I've wanted to quit, because the fight seemed endless, my heart kept saying not to give up on You. For You will never give up on me.

The Vessel

I am learning how to be Your vessel, Lord.

Yes, My vessel. There are parts of you that are broken, My child, but know this. You can hold water. Much water. My living water.

A lot of the time I do feel broken. But to have You tell me I can still hold water even during my times of weakness and troubles means everything to me, Jesus. I feel like You have come to me, in Your perfect time, and called me to be Your instrument, Your vessel for something I don't know yet. Something beyond myself awaits me.

Know that My providence prepares you for the work I have for you. And that the tools you will need will be provided. I want you to use the tools I give you. Here are some things you will need to know about a vessel. It needs to be cleaned out before it can contain something valuable and it is meant to contain something wonderful. A vessel needs to be emptied and filled. That is its function. The filling of the vessel contains Me, Your Holy Spirit. You are a chosen vessel for My work.

What You have said reminds me of this song. I want to sing it to You, Lord ...

    Spirit of the Living God, fall afresh on me.
    Spirit of the Living God, fall afresh on me.
    Melt me, mold me, fill me, use me.
    Spirit of the Living God, fall afresh on me.

       ~ Daniel Iverson, Song Lyrics ~

Oh, My child, you make Me dance with joy. You are My chosen vessel, for both now, and evermore.

Dark Night

Dark Night of My Soul

Father, I don't understand what I am going through right now. It feels heavy and foggy when I try to move through life like there is a dark cloud over my head. I feel tired and fatigued. Sadness sometimes overwhelms me to the point of severe sorrow that seems out of control. I'm in the worst state of being I've ever experienced in my life. I don't understand it nor can I seem to change it. What is happening to me, Lord?

Days seems to pass without awareness of You, Lord. I feel alone and lonely. Where are You, Jesus?

I am here, My child, though I know you are having trouble hearing Me or feeling My presence. There will be a time when you can. Here, take My manna for this day.

Sometimes, I want so badly to hear from You that it hurts when I don't. I know You are with me. You just seem so far away.

I am right here, dear one, right here. Take My living water and drink.

I feel depressed and sometimes anxious with no relief. I can barely cry out to You for help, yet when I do, it doesn't seem to come. How much longer, Lord? How much more can I bear?

You are strong, My daughter. So very strong. I will give you more strength as you need it. Take heart, you will hear My voice and feel My presence soon.

In my lifetime, I have been plagued by this depression, yet not known that's what it was. I want my soul to feel freedom yet it feels so tortured.

Where are You, Lord? Your silence is deafening. Just one word from You and I would feel something other than pain. One moment in Your presence would help lessen my sadness. Yet nothing comes.

Days pass into years. Have You been silent all these years concerning my pain or have I missed Your overtures in the midst of my fog?

Dear one, I am here. I have always been here just as I have promised. My silence was not meant to cause you further pain. In fact, My silence was not silence at all. I was working. Working on your behalf at all times. Never stopping. I was working underground. Under the soil of your life. Preparing something that needed to be planted, watered, and nurtured until it was time to unveil it to you. I was always with you. Always protecting you. Never letting you out of My arms. Your sorrow, hurt, frustration, and pain were Mine too. I felt what you felt, even more. What was hard for you to bear was hard for Me to bear. I did not want you to have to endure your struggle. Yet, I took what you were going through and turned it into something beautiful and useful. Though, it may not have felt like it, your endurance produced great strength within you. My dear one, you are stronger than you know. I know how strong you are and I want you to see that.

Oh, Father, I hear Your voice! Your lovely voice that melts my heart with just one whisper of a word. Oh, thank You, Jesus, for being my help. I looked for You and have found You.

Now it is time to show you what I have been preparing for you all these years. It is seeds of steady growth, each representing the strength needed to endure your struggle. Each one grows into another even stronger than before. It is you, dear one. It is who you are becoming, more and more of who I created you to be. I did not leave you in your struggle but protected you and was present with you at all times. I kept My promises to you, dear one. Always know I am faithful to My word. I am faithful to you.

In my mind's eye, I see something wonderful. I see You, Jesus. It is a picture of you and me during my dark night. You are covering me with Your embrace as a shield of protection. I have my back to You nestled in Your arms. I am safe and secure. Able to weather my storm. I'm realizing that You were protecting me just as You promised. This was all unseen to me during my dark night. Your work was underground. The love in Your protective embrace is what was giving me life. It is the strength of a father and the sweet embrace of a mother. I am the daughter, and have been ever since I was born.

Now, I realize the dark night was all about Your presence and my protection during what needed to take place for my growth. You were there. I can't get any closer to You right now, Lord. I feel so loved by You. I am learning that this is not a journey of getting closer to You but a journey of consciousness of You as You are always here.

My daughter, you are right about Me. For beneath your senses, I am instilling better love. It is about your transformation into being more like Me, more like love. You realize now the union between us that always existed during your struggles. I remember My first promises to you and I have always fulfilled them in your life. Now, I want to share something with you, dear one.

My name is Jehovah-Shammah.
I am always with you.

My name is Jehovah Roi.
I am your protector.

I love you dearly, My daughter.

[Later in my life, I found that the most common promise in the Bible is:

"I will be with you."]

Growth Emerges

†

"For as the soil makes the sprout come up and a garden causes seeds to grow, so the Sovereign Lord will make righteousness and praise spring up before all nations."

Isaiah 61:11
New International Version

My Shell

My Shell

Lord, why do I feel like I am in a shell? Unable to free myself from a prison I feel from within? There is something keeping me from being set free. It's tangible. I can feel it. My voice feels trapped and contained. Unable to speak and even if I did I would not know what to say. I feel troubled from within. There must have been a time when I was free? Can I remember it? All I feel is a soul wanting to break loose from the grip of something bigger than myself. Will I ever break free? Will I ever taste freedom?

Know this, My child, I am the lifter of your head. I am in your anxiety. I am in your shell. Freedom does await you.

"I am leaving you with a gift—peace of mind and heart. And the peace I give is a gift the world cannot give. So don't be troubled or afraid." (John 14:27 New Living Translation).

Wait for its coming. It will come, dear one. It will come. You will have a voice. Oh the things you will say! Wait for your freedom voice. It will come.

†

"But Lord, you are my shield,
my glory, and my only hope.
You alone can lift my head …"

Psalm 3:3
The Living Bible

The Ocean

I am feeling depressed, weighed down and worked over by life. You place before my mind an image. I see myself swimming out to sea and stopping to see where I am. I feel afraid because I can't believe I swam out this far. I have a fear of swimming in the ocean. I would not choose to swim in it. Yet, here I am. I panic with thoughts of drowning, sharks, or not being able to get back to shore. I can't believe I'm here. I want to get back to shore as fast as I can but I'm afraid if I do I will go back into that old depressed shell of mine. I almost would rather be out to sea than back in that shell. The feel of the ocean is cold, and the power of the waves make me feel vulnerable and helpless. How long must I stay out here?

It's been several weeks, Lord, and I believe I am out of the ocean. I learned some things from my ocean experience. I didn't get eaten by sharks like my fears tried to tell me. I didn't drown. I didn't go back to shore like my old self was inclined to do. I realized You were not going to miraculously take me out of the ocean to save me. You gave me the wisdom to float on my back when I got tired and wanted to give up. You gave me strength to look up from my position rather than around me, so I could see You and reach for You. When I finally said, "I give up, Lord. I can't do this on my own," I could let go of my fears and restraints and safely float into shore, not to escape my surroundings, but to be free from them.

I received a card today from a friend of mine. On the front was a black and white picture of three nuns joyfully running out of the water onto the beach. Lord, what makes this such a special gift is that my friend did not know the struggle I was enduring.

I love the way things work out for your good. Your friend was led to send you that very card. Enjoy your newfound freedom, dear one.

The Bud

I know I am sometimes in pain and hurting, so help me choose to bloom, Lord, even when I feel like I'm incapable of it.

I am here to help you, dear one. You are not alone in your pain and hurt. These things make you bloom with brilliance in the proper season.

Jesus, you are parting my blonde hair with Your hand. Like a mother does with her daughter.

You are My daughter, dear one. This is My constant love for you.

†

"And the day came when the risk to remain tight in a bud was more painful than the risk it took to bloom."

~ Anonymous ~

Lord, Prepare My Heart to Listen

Lord, I feel exhausted, but a good exhausted. My heart feels light and unburdened. You have taken me through the deepest parts of my soul for reflection, confession, struggles, and now relief. I need to be still now, Lord, so I can just hear from You, so that my mind, body, and spirit can relax and just be with You.

Your soul is beautiful, My child, and as beautiful, is your willingness to go beyond yourself. Now, it is time to just listen and receive from Me. Be still, dear one. Be still and know that I am God. Hear Me now.

†

"… call on me and come and pray to me, and I will listen to you."

Jeremiah 29:12
New International Version

Listening

✝

Holy Spirit, when I reflect on listening, I ask that You keep training my ear to hear Your lovely voice. So, speak Lord, for your servant is listening.

Listening

My Request

Lord, as I begin to listen for Your voice I have a request. I would like Your voice to be heard beyond my own knowledge or my own experience of You. Show me things I do not yet know. You are so much bigger than I can imagine. Help me to begin to understand so that I can open the box in which I sometimes keep you.

I am delighting in your request. Showing you how vast I am is something I love to do. Just wait and see what I am going to do. You will love it, My precious one.

Being Open

I want to open myself up to Your voice, Father. What is the best way to do that?

You don't have to fight for My voice. Just let it happen. It is to be received. What I desire, even before your words, is your heart. I see what's in your heart. When you are open, you also see. By seeing into your own heart, you are seeing Me. Then you will be open to Me.

†

"The Lord would speak to Moses face to face, as one speaks to a friend."

Exodus 33:11
New International Version

Your Beautiful Voice, Lord, I Do Hear

Lord, these are words I have thought about with You as we journal together. They are like snippets or partial thoughts that are in my heart about how I listen for Your voice.

Lord, I heard You say to me in Your gentle voice, *"Trust in Me for I trust in you."*

Lord, help me to listen today for the Holy Spirit's direction in whatever form it may be.

There is a lot going on around me so please don't let me lose sight of Your voice, Father.

As much as I believe in the power of prayer I believe equally in the power of listening. Lord, you have taught me both.

Thank You for the ability to listen, Lord. Never let me take it for granted.

The last several weeks have been full of listening opportunities. Did I miss any, Lord?

Father, I know that more listening and waiting is required.

Help me to never cease in listening for Your voice, Jesus.

You spoke to me today but why did it take so long before I heard You?

Lord, let me take the time to listen even when I have none.

Lord, here I am. Speak to me. And if You do and I don't hear You, speak to me until I do.

Listening to You now, Lord, has a different meaning for me. No longer do I listen just with my ears, but with every part of my body and all my senses.

I heard from within my soul, You saying to me, *"Watch what I can do if you give it all to Me!"*

I desire to hear Your voice. I want to be submissive so I can, and obedient when I do. This morning, as I am waking up, I pray that I will hear Your voice today, Holy Spirit.

Have I ever thought of the option that You may be trying to get my attention by *not* talking to me, Father?

Lord, I know You are here with me right now, as close as the air I breathe, face to face. You have been with me all night, keeping watch over my sleep, and hoping upon my awakening that I would still choose You. And I joyfully do, Lord.

I love when you tell Me your heart thoughts. They reach My ears with music of joy. Keep journaling. Keep listening. For I will keep speaking to you.

Another Way to Hear Your Voice

I recall some of my times with, You, God, not being all about words or silence. There is another aspect of You—a glimpse of something more being offered. Sometimes physical sensations occur within me. They have taken many forms, each having its own beauty. Pleasant is the sensation, never overbearing. It can be a steady flow of Your presence within my entire body that feels like a warm breeze on a spring day. It gets my attention and settles me into an intoxicating state of awareness of You.

There have been other sobering moments when I have been talking with someone that have felt like I was in Your presence. As we are talking, something suddenly changes in their face, not from their perspective, but from mine. Their words fade away, their eyes become still and intent on mine. At that very moment, I feel like I am looking at You, Jesus. You don't say anything. Your eyes, which I see through that person, say it all—love resides here. The moment seems to disappear quickly and I begin to hear the words of that person again.

I know that within these instances, You are using physical sensations so I will take notice of You and be drawn to You.

This is meant to show you how vast I am in communicating to you. I use all things to bring Myself to your attention. That is why the present moment is so important. I am in it and in it fully. I want you to be as well. There is so much to be seen in the present moment. Let's have fun together as we enjoy our moments together. We already do!

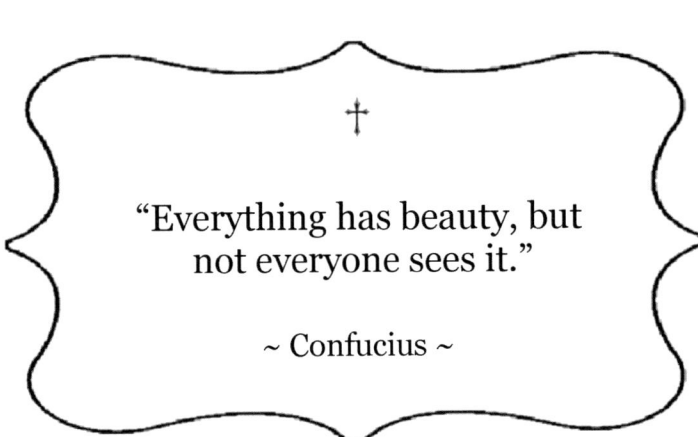

"Everything has beauty, but not everyone sees it."

~ Confucius ~

In My Favorite Chair

As I sit in my favorite chair, with my eyes closed, no distractions to divert my attention, no sounds to disrupt me, I think solely of You, Lord. It's just You and me at this moment. My concentration on You leads me deeper and deeper into a calm peace. My mind feels empty. My body feels a sensation of You slowly taking a warm blanket and wrapping me up in it from head to toe. I feel strengthened by Your warmth. It fills in all the dark, cold holes in my life. I feel Your strength filling me up. Then, at the perfect moment, You whisper to me,

Be comforted by My presence. My peace be with you, dear one. I leave you my peace.

Be Thou My Vision

Be thou my vision, O Lord of my heart;
naught be all else to me, save that thou art.
thou my best thought, by day or by night,
Waking or sleeping, thy presence my light.

Be thou my wisdom, and thou my true word;
I ever with thee and thou with me, Lord;
thou and thou only, first in my heart,
great God of heaven, my treasure thou art.

~ Ginny Owens, Mary E. Byrne, Song Lyrics ~

Acknowledge Me

L ord, I am seeking answers to a situation in my life. Help me understand. Make it clear to me, for I can't see.

Slowly and softly I hear,

Acknowledge Me for all I have done.

After talking with You, Lord, I decided to take my dog for a walk. I took a different route. I passed a car in a driveway that had a license plate with this Scripture verse on it,

"In all your ways acknowledge Him, and He shall direct your paths." (Proverbs 3:6 New King James Version).

Thank You, Jesus. I want to acknowledge You more and more. Help me know the ways I may not be. I know You will direct my paths.

The Silence of Listening

I just realized that for this whole prayer time I haven't said one word. You have done all the talking. I have enjoyed it immensely. One thing about Your voice, it's unique. You say things in a way that are so different than I am used to hearing in my own mind or from others. You speak in a tone that catches my attention even if it is softer than the other thoughts wondering around in my mind. I don't have to ask You to repeat Yourself. I seem to understand what You are saying to me as Your words resonate within my heart. Your voice is gentle, sweet and comforting even if You are making me aware of my sin. No matter what the words, I am always grateful for Your voice.

I am proud of you, dear one. Your ear is trained to recognize My voice. All the times we have spent together have produced your keen ear. There are so many competing voices for your attention. The world speaks. Evil speaks. And your own voice clamors in your mind. It is good to know how each one sounds so you can distinguish amongst them.

The world speaks of pleasure, wealth, and abundance. Evil lies and tries to trick you into temptation with things that could be better for you than what you already have. Confusion and vain glory are common tactics. Your own thoughts can be random meanderings that just clog your mind and make it hard to find clarity.

You are My sheep. My sheep know My voice and I lead them to where they need to go. You are My sheep and I am Your Shepherd. I will lead you, dear one, by My voice.

†

"They who dream by day are cognizant of many things which escape those who dream only by night."

~ Edgar Allan Poe ~

The Pond

Lord, I am beginning to see a pond in my mind. The pond is very small and intimate, surrounded by lush green grasses and tall trees. Beautiful flowers of all colors are flourishing here, shades I have not seen here on earth. Jesus, I see You standing on the water. All of creation recognizes You and expresses their excitement to see You.

I see You walking on the water until You reach the water's edge and then sit down on the bank. I can tell by the expression on Your face that You are in deep thought or contemplation. Then, You invite me to sit beside You and talk. You are willing to spend as much time with me as I need. We talk for a while about different things and then You get up and start walking away from the pond. I follow You until we reach a log that is in the grass. We sit there for a while and talk about some more things. Then You get up again, invite me to walk with You even further from the pond until we reach two trees that are shaped to form an entrance between them.

We walk through the entrance and see what looks like a field of gold that extends forever. It seems to have no end. I just stand there with You, Jesus, and marvel at it for a while, then follow You through it. It is waist-high wheat that feels like silk to my skin. It softly moves with the motion of our bodies walking through it and then returns to its original position behind us.

I begin to think. The pond is a place of extreme beauty, comfort, peace, and tranquility. I would like to spend more time there. It's a place I don't want to leave. Though, as I walk away from the pond, I discover this field of gold is even more beautiful than the pond. The possibilities are endless here. I can feel them. There is freedom here. I would not have known this if I had stayed at the pond.

What are you trying to tell me, Lord? What should I learn from this experience with You?

What do you think you have learned?

The pond scene was very beautiful and tranquil. I like that feeling and mostly want to stay in places like that. My heart resonates with it. But there are other places I can go that have just as much beauty, opportunity for growth, and adventure. This all awaits me as I venture out further and further away from what I am comfortable and content with. You are with me no matter where I go. Lord, lead me onward.

I love when you learn new things. Never stop inquiring. Never stop wanting to learn and grow. It makes your beauty stand out. And know this, there are times when you ask Me a question and My answer is simply, " What do you want?"

The Statues

Jesus, You are showing me an image of two statue-like people. They are clearly two distinct creations. One person looks like a statue made of a hard, white substance, like porcelain. You, Lord, are chipping away at it. It looks like You are spending a lot of time and effort to make the person look like You want. A lot of progress has been made but more needs to be done. You never give up on Your work before it is fully complete.

The other person is made of a darker clay-like substance, soft and pliable, like pottery clay. You are adding to their shape and defining their look. This statue appears easier to handle and shape. Yet, I can see that You are spending equal time on both statues. Both are created by the same artist and are being worked on by the same artist—You, God. Just in different ways.

I love everyone whom I've created. People with hearts more like porcelain need melting and patience. Those with hearts like clay are easier to lead. Shelly, you are the clay. And I will finish what I have started in you.

†

"I saw the angel in the marble and carved until I set her free."

~ Michelangelo ~

Trust

I am entering a small prayer chapel. It is empty as if You had planned for this time to be just between the two of us. It's a beautiful looking chapel with a large wooden cross off to the corner by itself. Nothing else is around it. Jesus, I feel You guiding me to Your cross with a force other than my own. My heart, mind, and soul are all responding as I walk closer and closer. I am standing before the cross now. I instinctively start to place all my belongings that I am carrying under it. First, my purse and coat, then my Bible and notebooks, all that is in my possession at this moment. Everything I have with me, Jesus, is now before You, at the foot of Your cross. Though I wasn't planning on doing it, I start to surrender everything I have to You, Jesus. It feels like I no longer need anything to satisfy me right now. All I need is You, Jesus.

"Is there anything more I need to do, my Lord?"

The answer comes back quickly.

Trust that what I have done for you on the cross is enough. What needed to be done has been done. It is good to surrender. To surrender all. When I died on the cross it gave you life. Every time you surrender, remember what I gave up so that you may have life, and have it abundantly. Now, live.

Lord, Prepare My Heart to Give You Thanks

All I can do right now is give You my heart that is overflowing with thanksgiving. I feel ready and desiring to give back to You all that You have given to me. I know You are deserving of so much more but I will give You all that I have.

Tell me of your thankfulness towards Me, dear one. We can celebrate together.

Thanksgiving

✝

Father, when I reflect on thanksgiving,
I joyfully consider how I can bless You
for how You have blessed me.
Love that thought.

Dance of Thanksgiving

Thanking God Through Scripture

Lord, you have blessed me so greatly through Your Word that I want to bless You by writing down the ways I am thankful for it. There are many!

"Make a joyful shout to the Lord, all you lands! Serve the Lord with gladness; Come before His presence with singing. Know that the Lord, He is God; It is He who has made us, and not we ourselves; We are His people and the sheep of His pasture. Enter into His gates with thanksgiving, And into His courts with praise. Be thankful to Him, and bless His name." (Psalm 100 New King James Version).

"Let me shout God's name with a praising song. Let me tell his greatness in a prayer of thanks." (Psalm 69:30 The Message).

"I will give thanks to you, Lord, with all my heart; I will tell of all your wonderful deeds." (Psalm 9:1 New International Version).

"Let us come before him with thanksgiving and extol him with music and song. For the Lord is the great God, the great King above all gods." (Psalm 95:2-3 New International Version).

"Give thanks to the Lord, for he is good; his love endures forever." (1 Chronicles 16:34 New International Version).

"I will give thanks to the Lord because of his righteousness; I will sing the praises of the name of the Lord Most High." (Psalm 7:17 New International Version).

I meant for My Word to bless you and I am delighted that it brings you such joy. Thankfulness is such a heart cleanser, softener, and joy giver. Keep it coming, dear one. I am blessed by you.

Thanking God from My Heart

All I can do right now, Lord, is shout out my love for You from my heart. My heart of thanksgiving. Here goes, Father!

Thank You for never letting me go!

Thank You for directing my path. You are my Light!

Thank You for making me feel special and loved!

Thank You for continued chances. I know they are bottomless but I don't ever want to take them for granted!

Thank You for the desires You have placed in my heart. They let me see more of You!

Thank You for making me feel so safe and secure in Your arms!

Thank You for the ways You love me!

Thank You for Your peace inside of me that I can draw on in times of need!

Thank You for the sunrise this morning. It helped me see the beauty of starting a new day!

Thank You for the oak tree in our backyard. I love the way it brings filtered shade to my day!

Thank You for the fresh summer berries this morning. They made me stop and taste goodness!

Thank You for the barefoot walk on our grass. It made me feel grounded to the earth You have created!

Thank You for the changing of seasons. It makes me in tune with the changing seasons of my soul!

Thank You for the incredible pink and purple colors of the sunset tonight. You are the artist!

Thank You for the puffy white cloud formations today in the brilliant blue sky. I could daydream all day!

Thank You for the calming beauty of water. It never ceases to sooth my soul!

Thank You, Lord, for my children. They bring out so much of You to me!

Thank You for my puppies. Their gentle spirits help me find mine!

Thank You for the details of flowers. That You would go to such lengths to design a flower. How much more You love us in all our complexity!

Thank You for my heartbeat. I love life!

Thank You for this day. I get to be with You!

Thank You for my husband. He makes me feel secure in his arms!

Thank You for the prayers of joy and thanks in my heart. Sometimes they are subtle and other times they are accompanied by trumpets!

Thank You, Lord, for Your Holy Spirit in my life. He is the tap on my shoulder and the whisper in my ear I have been praying for!

Thank You for Your arms that hold me. You are my love embrace!

There is so much to be thankful for I'm glad to say I will be thanking You into eternity!

Thank You for giving me more chances even when I fail. You love me that much!

Thank You for saving me. Thank You for showing me I needed to be saved. I will never forget what You have done for me, Jesus!

I hear them, dear one. They are shouts of beautiful thanksgiving to My ears. I love every one. They are a precious reflection of who I created you to be. I want you to notice that, My daughter, for you are beautiful to Me.

"Gratitude paints little smiley faces on everything it touches."

~ Richelle E. Goodrich ~

Lord, Prepare My Heart for Endings

Lord, I don't know what the future holds. I only know my heart is full right now in this moment. Help me to keep the desires of my heart close at hand. Some are about the future and some are for the present moments that I don't want to pass unnoticed. I pray I will take notice of Your never-ending presence in my life and Your voice that guides me along in the present, moving me towards my future.

I have an invitation for you, dear one. It is about what lies ahead for you. Listen for it. It will flow gently into your heart. I am excited for you to receive My invitation. It will bring us both joy.

Endings

✝

Jesus, as I contemplate endings to this chapter of my life, I'm sensing mine as an invitation to a new beginning.
An exciting thought.

†

"Your path has been both broken and beautiful and just as it was supposed to be."

~ Unknown ~

My Tapestry

This is what I have learned. My relationship with You, Jesus, started to become real to me through the pages of my journal. It was a relationship of prayer and always has been.

What I've learned is that this relationship has been beautifully orchestrated to paint a picture of an exquisite tapestry. There are knots, twists and turns, frayed and rough edges on the back of the tapestry. It can be a bit of a mess. It shows me being worn and worn out, sometimes appearing to mean nothing, making no sense or having no form. But the back of the tapestry is what makes the front so exquisite.

And now, I can start to see how all this was designed to make the beautiful artwork on the other side—the amazing artwork of a long-term prayer relationship with You, my Jesus. Showing beauty and clarity of purpose of who I really am.

My dear one, look at the back of your tapestry. I know you see a mess but that's not what I see. Don't try and change the look of the back of the tapestry. What really matters is not what the back looks like but what holds it all together. And I am what holds it all together. It is there you find the real meaning of the tapestry.

The Tapestry

When we embrace the many parts of our experience we discover a magnificent creation. Every moment is but a thread, a thread of consciousness embracing the very essence of life. Some threads are brilliant and dazzling while others are tattered and torn. When looked upon in isolation the tattered threads look inferior. Yet when woven together by the wondrous hands of the Creator, the light magically blends with the dark. As joy coalesces with pain God creates the magnificent tapestry that is life.

~ Debbie Milam ~

✝

"You will go out in joy and be led forth in peace; the mountains and hills will burst into song before you, and all the trees of the field will clap their hands."

Isaiah 55:12
New International Version

Meadow on the Ledge

Meadow on the Ledge

Lord, this is the picture You are giving me now of myself after I've been through my journaling of worship, prayer, confession, struggles, listening, and thanksgiving. The picture is of a meadow on the ledge, which is what my name, "Shelly" means.

Father, help me visualize what a meadow on the ledge looks like. I can see something forming in my mind. It looks like a window ledge growing out of a rocky cliff. From the rocks and rubble, is growing a beautiful, colorful garden. It amazes me that this is even possible. I think that's what makes it so spectacular.

The illustration, meadow on the ledge, is a perfect picture of where I've been. The rocky, underground, dark rubble parts of my life are now redeemed into something beautiful and flourishing—a garden. Though my path has been broken, that's the beauty.

I hear you call me by name.

Shelly ...

"Arise, shine for your light has come, and the glory of the Lord rises upon you." (Isaiah 60:1 New International Version).

"See, I am doing a new thing! Now it springs up; do you not perceive it?" (Isaiah 43:19 New International Version).

This is your meadow on the ledge, dear one. Look around. There are no other "Shellys" here. This is all yours. Look some more and notice, what was underground is now visible and flourishing.

The meadow of lush flowers is you. Your voice has come forth. You have come forth. You are you. You are beautiful. And the world sees you.

Lord, I am walking the pathway to the upper meadow on the ledge. I am falling in love with You all over again. Jesus, You are telling me a love story. Our love story. From in the beginning ...

This is how I feel about you, Shelly, My meadow on the ledge ...

I call you by name. I lay My hands upon you. I knit you together. You are wonderfully made. I know every hair on your head. You are precious and honored. You are a crown of splendor in My hands. My banner over you is love. I rejoice over you with singing. I take great delight in you. You are the apple of My eye. I am ever before you. My glory rises upon you. You are rarer than fine gold. I gaze upon you. I have engraved you upon the palms of My hands. I behold you.

Tell me again of Your love for me, Jesus!

I will for eternity, My beloved!

Beyond the Trees

Beyond the Trees

Lord, what's out there beyond the trees? What's out there for the two of us?

Come and see. Let's go together and I'll take you there. I will never lead you away from My voice. I will always be with you. I will always protect you. I can't wait to show you, My beloved, beyond the trees, what's out there for the two of us.

I wonder what my journaling will be like beyond the trees? It's been such a large part of my relationship with You and I don't want to lose it or my love for it. I feel like maybe something new is going to happen for me beyond the trees. What, I don't know. But I can feel something stirring in me that leads me to believe our relationship is going to go even deeper than I can imagine. And what a feeling that is!

Take your journal, My beloved. It is yours forever. Don't stop journaling. It is a gift to you and Me. Though, you are right, I am stirring in you. There is something new going to happen beyond the trees. And it will deepen our relationship even more. Imagine it. Yes, imagine it, My dear one. Hold your journal and let's go together ... to a new beginning made especially for you, My beloved.

Lord, Prepare My Heart for New Beginnings

This makes me want to sing to You, Father.

> Jesus, Jesus, Jesus! There's just something about that name!
>
> Master, Savior, Jesus! Like the fragrance after the rain.
>
> Jesus, Jesus, Jesus! Let all heaven and earth proclaim.
>
> Kings and kingdoms will all pass away, but there's something about that name!
>
> ~ Gloria Gaither,
> William J. Gaither, Song Lyrics ~

Shelly, My dear one, you are prepared for your new beginning. Beyond the trees ...

Offerings to Ponder

Find a comfortable place to spend some quiet time with God, to ponder the following questions. These questions are my offerings to you should you desire to contemplate how each chapter of this book relates to you. Use them as you wish. Consider journaling your thoughts as a way to become more aware of your closeness with God and experiences with Him. My prayer is that you may receive inspiration from this book to further your own personal journey with God.

Beginnings
1. Did God reveal anything to you after reading this chapter?
2. Do you feel God leading you to a new beginning in your life? Can you visualize it?
3. Do you have a question to ask God after reading this chapter?

Praise
1. What word best describes your feelings after reading this chapter?
2. How could you express these feelings to God?

Prayer
1. What about prayer do you find appealing?
2. Do you sense the presence of God through prayer?
3. What would you like Jesus to say to you about prayer?

Confession
1. Describe your awareness of God's presence after reading this chapter?
2. How do you feel about confession being a conversation with God?
3. If you feel the need for confession, how do you think God will respond?

Struggles
1. What is your soul longing for today?
2. What do you think the Spirit of God may be whispering to you right now?
3. How would you like God to touch your soul?

Thanksgiving
1. How is your heart towards God today?
2. How could you express that to Him?
3. What qualities of God's love come alive for you in this moment?

Endings
1. After reading this book, what emotions best describe how you are feeling?
2. With which chapter did you most resonate? Why?
3. Did God whisper to you any invitations to start, stop or change something in your life?
4. What has God taught you about His presence and experiencing Him in deeper ways?
5. What may be *your* new beginning?
6. What is your most significant take away from this book?

Scripture References

Scripture quotations taken from the Amplified® Bible (AMP), Copyright © 2015 by The Lockman Foundation. Used by permission. www.Lockman.org

THE HOLY BIBLE, NEW INTERNATIONAL VERSION®, NIV® Copyright © 1973, 1978, 1984, 2011 by Biblica, Inc.® Used by permission. All rights reserved worldwide.

The Living Bible copyright © 1971 by Tyndale House Foundation. Used by permission of Tyndale House Publishers Inc., Carol Stream, Illinois 60188. All rights reserved. The Living Bible, TLB, and the The Living Bible logo are registered trademarks of Tyndale House Publishers.

Scripture quotations are from the Revised Standard Version of the Bible, copyright © 1946, 1952, and 1971 the Division of Christian Education of the National Council of the Churches of Christ in the United States of America. Used by permission. All rights reserved.

Scripture taken from The Message. Copyright © 1993, 1994, 1995, 1996, 2000, 2001, 2002. Used by permission of NavPress Publishing Group.

Scripture quotations are taken from the Holy Bible, New Living Translation, copyright © 1996, 2004, 2015 by Tyndale House Foundation. Used by permission of Tyndale House Publishing, Inc., Carol Stream, Illinois 60188. All rights reserved.

The ESV® Bible (The Holy Bible, English Standard Version®). ESV® Text Edition: 2016. Copyright © 2001 by Crossway, a publishing ministry of Good News Publishers. The ESV® text has been reproduced in cooperation with and by permission of Good News Publishers. Unauthorized reproduction of this publication is prohibited. All rights reserved.

Contemporary English Version® Copyright © 1995 American Bible Society. All rights reserved.

Scripture taken from The Expanded Bible. Copyright © 2011 by Thomas Nelson. Used by permission. All rights reserved.

Scripture is taken from GOD'S WORD®, © 1995 God's Word to the Nations. Used by permission of Baker Publishing Group.

Scriptures taken from the KING JAMES VERSION (KJV): KING JAMES VERSION, public domain.

Scripture taken from the New King James Version®. Copyright © 1982 by Thomas Nelson. Used by permission. All rights reserved.

Poems, Songs, and Quote References

Beginnings

Father's Embrace, poem. Stuart Townend. Copyright © 2007 Thankyou Music (PRS) (adm. Worldwide at CapitolCMGPublishing.com). All rights reserved. Used by permission.

Behold our God, song. Jonathon Baird, Megan Baird, Ryan Baird, Stephen Altrogge. Copyright © 2011 Sovereign Grace Worship (ASCAP) Sovereign Grace Praise (BMI) (adm. At CapitalCMGPublishing.com). All rights reserved. Used by permission.

Confession

Ointment Poured Forth, quote. Wonderful Names of Our Wonderful Lord, by Charles Hurlburt and T. C. Horton, © 1998 Barbour Publishing, Inc. Used by permission.

Struggles

Spirit of the Living God, song. Daniel Iverson. Copyright © 1994 Birdwing Music (ASCAP) (adm. At Capital CMGPublishing.com) / Hope Publishing Company (ASCAP). All rights reserved. Used by permission.

Listening

Be Thou My Vision, song. Ginny Owens, Mary E. Bryne. Copyright © 1999 Universal Music–Brentwood Benson Publishing (ASCAP) (adm. At CapitalCMGPublishing.com). All rights reserved. Used by permission.

Thanksgiving

Richelle E. Goodrich, quote. Permission courtesy of Richelle E. Goodrich.

Endings

The Tapestry, poem. Debbie Milam. Permission courtesy of Debbie Milam.

There's Something About That Name, song. Gloria Gaither, William J. Gaither. Copyright © 1970 Hanna Street Music (BMI) (adm. At CapitalCMGPublishing.com). All rights reserved. Used by permission.

Made in the USA
Lexington, KY
02 May 2018